# Harrison

THE BOY WHO WOULD NEVER RUN

# Harrison

## The Boy Who Would Never Run

by Harrison Shetlin
with Dr. R. Jay Shetlin

Published by
RockStar Publishing House
32129 Lindero Canyon Road, Suite 205
Westlake Village, CA 91361
www.rockstarpublishinghouse.com

Author Shetlin, Dr. R. Jay
    Harrison
    ISBN:
    Paperback: 9781937506827
    eBook: 9781937506834

Cover design by: Michael Short
Cover photo: Shutterstock.com
Interior design: Scribe, Inc.
All images courtesy of the author

www.shetlin.com
www.drjayshetlin.com

# CONTENTS

# Me and My 12<sup>th</sup> Birthday

Hi, I'm Harrison! This weekend is my 12<sup>th</sup> Birthday. That may not sound like a big deal to you, but to me, it is nothing shy of a miracle. Why, you ask? Because I barely survived my first three days of life on earth. After my brush with death I was left with health challenges that would make even the simplest of daily tasks an absolute chore, or physically impossible! Yet here I am, 12 years old, healthy, happy, and, as far as anyone can tell, just a normal kid. (I am sure my siblings would disagree.)

Here is my story of life, near-death and overcoming insurmountable odds through the power of prayer, faith, nutrition, chiropractic care and the loving support of family. This is my story of, "The Boy Who Would Never Run."

# CHAPTER 1

# My First Weekend

"It was Saturday night April 6th, 2002." My dad has told the story so many times that I feel like I was there. That's right, I was . . . But I was only a day and a half old at the time. ☺ "Baby Harrison (that's me) had a smooth and trouble-free home birth." Well, as trouble-free as birth can be. I'm only 12 years old and don't know much about it, but I have yet to hear any woman say it is fun. Anyway, there seemed to be no reason for trouble with mine. Yet, here I was, just a day and a half old and I was very sick. I was not eating well, light bothered me, and the slightest movements made me wince in pain. Even though I have been curled up in the fetal position for the last nine months, my body would extend or arch backwards. To my dad, who is a chiropractic physician, these were all very concerning signs.

Mom was getting nervous. With her postpartum hormones in full swing, she could hardly keep from crying with concern for my well-being. Even with the support of visiting family, including her mom and dad, my mom wanted to cradle and kiss me to full health. But unfortunately, every touch hurt.

Call it "Murphy's Law" but for some reason we kids like to get sick late at night and on the weekends. I may have been new to this world, but I too followed this law to a "T." It had to be around 11 p.m. when Dad first started to piece the diagnosis together . . . fever, not eating, wincing in pain and extension dominant . . . the likelihood of it being serious was at the top of his mind.

Dad slipped and said, "Boy, he is showing some of the signs of meningitis." The words escaped his lips before his conscious filter realized the panic this could cause in the family. You see, my mom, who is without a doubt one of the sweetest people you could ever have the pleasure of meeting on this planet, is completely deaf due to the spinal meningitis she had when she was just two-and-a-half years old. Yep, she has not heard a single sound since that age. Because of the meningitis, she almost died, literally! She was so close to death that the doctors gave up on her and told Grandma and Grandpa that their daughter (my mom) would probably not make it through the night. They had tried every treatment and antibiotic known at that time. In fact, the family story goes, that when Great-Grandpa heard she was seriously ill, he fasted and prayed for three days then drove several hours up to the hospital to offer a special bed-side prayer or blessing on baby Shannon (my mom) the night she was supposed to die. Miraculously, and to the doctors' surprise, she lived through the night and slowly regained her strength. But, she never heard another sound, and she even had to be potty trained all over again. It really set her back! The cascade of challenges to follow this one simple, yet devastating illness, affected the entire family from that point forward.

Dad realized what he had just said could cause a flood of unwanted fear and emotion anchored to his wife and in-law's previous experience. He blurted, "Or it could just be one of many simple things. We will call the pediatrician in the morning to make sure everything is okay."

Thanks to me (I guess) we all had a pretty sleepless night. First thing Sunday morning Dad called the pediatrician and explained my symptoms. Concerned, the pediatrician replied, "I will meet you at the ER in 15 minutes."

Mom, Dad and I loaded up in our car and headed to the St. George Hospital. St. George, Utah is a quaint little town just six miles north of Utah's southernmost border, about ninety minutes north of Las Vegas, Nevada, on Interstate 15. A desert oasis with lots of red dirt and scenic mesas, everything in town takes fifteen minutes to get to as there are no straight lines to anywhere. There seems to be a butte, mesa or tortoise habitat between any two destinations.

Upon arrival my dad hastily met with the pediatrician to discuss my condition. As my dad feared, the MD also thought spinal meningitis was a strong probability and needed to be ruled out.

What's the big deal with meningitis, you ask? From what I hear, viral is not fun, but bacterial can be deadly within forty-eight hours! Dad tells me there are twenty-four strands of bacterial meningitis and eight of them are deadly.

Luckily, I don't remember this because it sounds painful . . . The pediatrician placed me on a small medical roller table and left momentarily to get the necessary testing equipment. When he returned he instructed my dad to hold my feet to my face and head. This forced my spine into a "C" curve or fetal position to spread my spine bones apart. What happened next I wouldn't wish on anybody . . . the Pediatrician stuck a surprisingly large needle in my back and began drawing out my spinal fluid

Dad tells me that after just a few cc's of fluid, he and the pediatrician looked at each other, and without a single spoken word, they knew there was a big problem. Cerebral spinal fluid circulates around the brain and spinal cord about every two hours. Its job is to help suspend the delicate nerve tissue; protect it from impact, among other things. It is supposed to be a clear fluid. Mine was "milky white" which means it was full of bacteria and fighter white "T" cells, or immune system cells.

Dad knew on sight that I was fighting an epic bacterial infection. He quickly did the math in his head. It had been about thirty-six hours since he first saw signs and symptoms of my battle with spinal meningitis. Dad looked at the pediatrician, who said, "We don't have time to test this to see which strand of bacterial this is, so we have to get this kid on every heavy-hitter antibiotic right now, or he is not going to live to see tomorrow."

# CHAPTER 2

# Life and Death at the Hospital

As I was wheeled away to a prep room, my dad was left standing holding the list of antibiotics I would be taking over the next twenty-one days (If I survived that long). He read the label of these strong and potentially life-saving drugs, which included their side effects. Several were listed, but three of them really caught Dad's attention, "May cause hearing problems, including permanent deafness. May cause kidney problems. May cause permanent motor neurological problems, known as cerebral palsy."

Dad thought how Mom is lucky to be alive, and how she has not heard a thing since her run in with spinal meningitis. Dad worried for a moment about this and the other two big side effects, but thought, "I have met several people in the past who have battled with meningitis and had little or no residual negative effects. Statistically, if Harrison survives, he has better than a 50% chance that he won't have any of these side effects to deal with." So Dad changed his focus to just saving my life and dealing with other challenges on the upside when I lived through the treatments.

Being a baby, I didn't get an arm IV but "a pic line." That is where they put an IV in your foot, or your scalp.

I guess this would make it easier for nurses to administer the antibiotics four times per day over the next twenty-one days. Mom was really troubled by the sight of me with all these monitoring wires and a big needle in my head. But this is what modern medicine had to offer, and it was my best chance for survival.

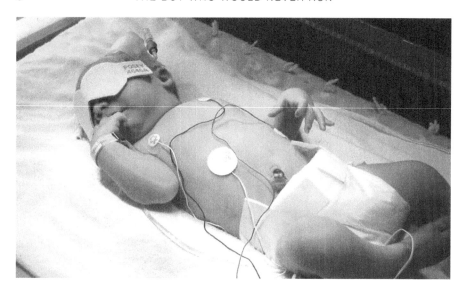

Things were going well after seven days in the hospital. I was still alive! I seemed to be making good progress.

Dad was checking on the insurance and carefully making sure our family wouldn't get stung with crazy unexpected medical expenses. It was costing around $4000 per day for me to stay in the hospital, and it was really stressful on the family going back and forth. It turned out our insurance informed my dad that I wasn't covered because we had started with this insurance company the month after Mom was already pregnant with me.

The concern of mounting medical bills led my dad to talk with the hospital. Even though his specialty does not allow for working in prescription drugs, since Dad was a physician the hospital granted permission to continue administering the antibiotics from home to help save on the cost. So, after seven days in the hospital, I was able to move to the comfort of home and continue with my treatments. Nurses would deliver more antibiotics once a week. Mom or Dad would carefully give them to me through my arm IV.

After the twenty-one days of antibiotics being completed there was an air of relief in the home. A "Whew, we did it. Harrison is going to be all right." Lucky for me, I was still around and seemingly better every day.

Dad had been on the phone with the hospital and the insurance, trying to work out the finances of my now, "saved life."
The cost to date was $26,000, which could have easily been
closer to $80,000 had I stayed the full time in the hospital.
(Hey, I know I'm not cheap, but I'm worth it!) We just had to
chalk it up to "the cost of success."

But how successful were we?

# CHAPTER 3

# The 2-Month Check-up

Over the weeks to come I seemed to be eating better and doing okay. My dad noticed a few oddities, like my eyes were always rolled up in my head. I wouldn't bring them down to try and look at things or track movement. I didn't seem to care. I guess I was just glad to still be around, basking in the love and embrace commonly given me by my family.

Dad was worried, but knew we had a check-up in a few weeks with the pediatrician. Dad did a lot of the "what if" research, trying to find out what he should do to help me, depending on the variety of outcomes possible either from leftover problems due to the meningitis or side effects of the heavy medications I had to take.

**The Two Month Check-up**

The time soon came where I was supposed to return to see the pediatrician for my two month "well baby" check-up. Naturally, we would review the happenings since the time at the hospital on my 3$^{rd}$ day of life to current, and I guess the doctor measured me to see how I was growing, suggested vaccines, etc.

It was much nicer to visit the pediatrician's office vs. the ER. It was more kid friendly with colors and little tables and toys. Not that I remember that either, but that is what I am told. My mom and dad took me into one of the exam rooms where a nurse measured how long or tall I was getting. "Check," that was good. She put me on a scale and measured my weight. Again, "Check," that was within expected normal.

The nurse left the room, and as far as we could see, things were looking good.

After a few minutes the doctor entered the room. He walked with a bit of a limp. Hmm, I guess I didn't notice that before. My dad and he spoke for a few minutes. Dad mentioned how things went with the full course of antibiotics at home, how I was sleeping and the few odd characteristics he noticed I did regularly. For example, I still liked to stretch back or arch my back, my eyes did not track well, and just a few other things. The doctor listened intently, and jotted down a few notes in my chart. Hmm, only one of his arms worked right. The left one seems "gimpy;" I guess I didn't notice that before either. Well, you know what they say, with age comes wisdom and awareness. The doctor rubbed his chin with his good hand as he looked at me being held in my dad's arms, thinking and studying my wiggles. He asked my dad to put me on the exam table, and with his good hand he unwrapped the stethoscope from around his neck and awkwardly walked the two steps to get close enough to me to perform his well-baby exam. I'm not sure what he noticed, maybe it was my imbalance and spastic

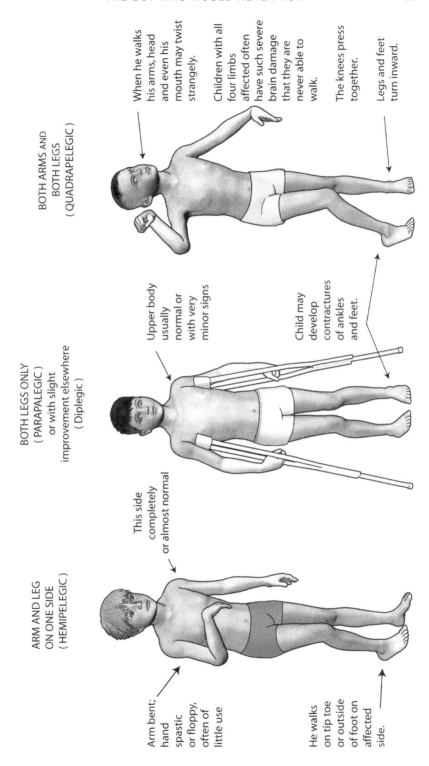

**BOTH ARMS AND BOTH LEGS ( QUADRAPELEGIC )**

When he walks his arms, head and even his mouth may twist strangely.

Children with all four limbs affected often have such severe brain damage that they are never able to walk.

The knees press together.

Legs and feet turn inward.

**BOTH LEGS ONLY ( PARAPALEGIC ) or with slight improvement elsewhere ( Diplegic )**

Upper body usually normal or with very minor signs

Child may develop contractures of ankles and feet.

**ARM AND LEG ON ONE SIDE ( HEMIPELEGIC )**

This side completely or almost normal

Arm bent; hand spastic or floppy, often of little use

He walks on tip toe or outside of foot on affected side.

muscle movement in my limbs, maybe it was the eyes rolled in my head, maybe it was my charming good looks and adorable baby fat, I don't know, but something caused him to step back, rub his face some more in deep thought then finally, to posture. Yes, the posture someone takes at that moment they are going to break you the bad news. My dad recognized it right away and thought, "Here it comes."

The pediatrician was careful to make eye contact with each of my parents as he stated their names compassionately, yet firmly to be sure and hold their attention and so my mom could read his lips. "Shannon," he paused and looked at my dad, "Jay" then looking back at Mom to finish his thought, "You two are going to have to prepare yourselves because this kid is just not right. What I mean is, he will be smart, but he will not have coordinated motor skills. He will eventually be able to walk, but stairs are going to be difficult. Riding a bike, forget about it. It looks like he has a severe case of cerebral palsy."

Mom didn't know what to think. Dad's mind raced through what he had been taught in diagnostics class at Chiropractic College and his life experience of people he had met with cerebral palsy. He remembered when he was twenty-two, living and going to college in California. He was roommates with an older man he knew from church. His roommate, Jim, was in his 30's, hard of hearing and a brilliant accountant. He remembered Jim explaining that at birth the cord was wrapped around his neck, apparently resulting in his condition of cerebral palsy. Jim walked with an altered gait, head tilted and a retracted arm.

As Dad thought about it he realized both his former roommate and the pediatrician who stood before him now suffered the same challenges. They were both smart enough to receive college educations and provide for their families with promising careers, but there were obvious physical challenges and limitations that the average person didn't have. Dad was taking a mental inventory of what limits I might have and what possibilities were still wide open for me. As for me, I still didn't know what they were talking about. In fact, I was still so "floppy" that I couldn't even hold my head up, let alone focus my eyes on anyone.

My condition was discussed for only a few minutes then the subject turned back to "well-baby check-up" topics. The pediatrician had seen my older siblings and knew how my dad felt about vaccines, but brought the topic anyway. Mom and Dad were still mentally dazed by the recent bombshell regarding my CP. Dad paused a minute, as if to fully process all the new data with his old programming. He looked up at my pediatrician and humbly said, "Well doc, if this is a neurological disorder, and I want to give Harrison any chance at overcoming it to the best of his ability, then I need to keep his nervous system free of ANY toxins such as the heavy metals, Aluminum, Mercury and other nerve toxic agents we use as preservatives in the vaccines. I think we will pass."

I'm no doctor (yet :+) but I am sure the pediatrician has all the reasons in his head why he believes vaccines are good for kids. Just like my dad with his physician training has all the reasons in his head why they are not good for kids.

As we headed home that day, Dad was multi-tasking. He was both driving and prayerfully asking, "Why do I have this kid? Is there a reason he and his challenges were given to me? Are my life experience, my medical training, and my holistic thinking something that will help or hinder this child?" He pondered and prayed the entire time. Dad tells me that it was along the drive home that he had felt a strong impression upon his mind. Some might call it a spiritual experience, a still small voice or a whisper. Whatever it was it left an undeniable impression on my dad saying, "Jay, you know what you need to do. Just do it, and be patient. It will work in Harrison's time, not your time."

You see, Dad had learned a recipe for health that has worked wonders on so many people, his patients. He had not been using that recipe on me, but now he was about to start, and I am glad he did!

For the previous two months, or my entire life to that point, Dad was just that, "Dad." He wasn't being "a doctor" for me. He would hand me over to other doctors and nurses asking, "What can you do to help my child?" He simply was not in doctor mode when it came to me. That was about to change.

# CHAPTER 4

# My Parents: Hippies or Healers?

Before I go much further with my own story, I should probably tell you a little about my parents and my siblings. I think this is important because some of the choices that seriously altered the course of my life were based on the sum of life experienced of my family before I arrived.

## Mom

My mom was born in the town of Bountiful, Utah. You already know her bout with spinal meningitis and how that set her back in her normal toddler development. Her parents took her to a number of specialists to find out how they could best help her grow and have as "normal" of life as possible. There was a great amount of pressure for her to go to a deaf school and learn sign language, but the test found that Mom would be able to learn to read lips, and with the right speech therapist, she would be able to speak pretty well. My dad talks about her in his book, "Solving the Health and Wealth Conundrum," and how even with this great disability, she would spend the summer learning to read lips to the vocabulary she would need her next year in school. She would sit in the front row of class and do her best to read the lips of the teacher. If she was lucky, she would get 40% of what was being said and just have to fill in the rest as best as she could. Kids are tough critics of other kids. She had plenty of teasing and ridicule at school, but not hearing what was said, she grew with a good positive attitude. Later she went to a dance class with one of her friends, and the desire was sparked to join a dance team. Grandma helped her join a "Stars" drill team, where she learned to synchronize her dance skills with several other girls, all without hearing a single beat of the music. As she grew, she continued this skill through high school. Her high school drill team even took State two years in a row while she was on the team. For a time, she performed in college with the Weber State College drill team and the University of Utah Drill Team. My dad says one of the miracles of Mom's positive attitude is that because she can't hear, she hasn't been exposed to as much of the negative rhetoric that the rest of us are exposed to every day. Mom eventually did learn sign language just before she met my dad. Unfortunately, I learned sign language as my first language, but quickly forgot it once I figured out she could read my lips.

**Dad**

My dad moved around a lot growing up. He was born in San Diego, California, but after his parents split, he and my grandma Fran ended up in Spokane, Washington, while my grandpa Fred settled in the Seattle area. In the 4th grade Dad was big on his favorite TV show, "The Incredible Hulk," staring Lou Ferrigno. In a freak accident, Dad was shocked by a large dose of electricity that knocked him to the ground several feet back from where he was standing. As he brushed himself off and got back to his feet, his young mind processed the accident as something similar to being Gamma-rayed much like Bruce Banner in the Hulk. Thus was born his desire for health and fitness. You see, young Dad thought that if he was more muscular when he wasn't angry, when his anger flared he would be even stronger. Yeah, I agree with what you are thinking—what a nut! It took him a few years to realize (grow out of the idea) that he was, in fact, not a mini hulk. Regardless, he could do 240 push-ups a day in the 4th grade ☺. When dad was in the fifth grade, Grandma Fran was in a car accident and Dad went with her several times to her chiropractic appointments. She would tell him how much better she felt after the treatments, which left an impression on Dad's mind. He decided then that he would be a chiropractic physician when he grew up.

While Dad was starting Jr. High, he and Grandma Fran moved to Layton, Utah. At the end of 8th grade several of the local schools have "Lagoon Day" where kids are bused to the local amusement park, Lagoon (Picture a Six-flags park in Utah). Mom and Dad actually met for the first time at the infamous "Lagoon Day." From what Dad tells me, he and his friend from Layton met up with Mom and her friend from Bountiful, and the four of them hung-out together for part of the day. Dad says he was the "5th wheel" as both the girls really liked his friend. Mom's story is a little different.

They never saw each other again until some twelve years later as Dad was finishing up his undergrad studies at the University of Utah, where he was also working at the U of U hospital as a research assistant in the OB/GYN department. He was nearly finished and preparing to move to Davenport, Iowa, for Medical/Chiropractic studies at Palmer College of Chiropractic.

Dad and Mom both happened to be at a deaf church youth activity where they saw each other in passing. A friend set them up on a date later that week, and the rest is history. Just a few short months later, they both moved to Davenport where our family began.

After their first year of marriage and graduate school, my sister, Savanna was born. Mom says she had my sister the regular way, meaning at the hospital, yadda yadda. (I'm really bored telling you this, but it is important to understand how my parents did stuff for me.) Anyway, super long labor. Thirty-eight hours, I am told. Nurses running around like they needed to remove a tumor. The doctor was a nice guy with a great reputation, but was in a hurry and wanted to cut and induce with drugs. Bottom line, it was a tough experience on Mom.

Before Mom got pregnant with my brother Josh, she did some research and decided to have a nurse mid-wife. In Iowa, the nurse mid-wives have hospital privileges at a birthing center attached to the hospital, so it is a more comfortable environment, with the safety of emergency facilities just down the hall. (Not a bad idea) That seemed to work well for Mom. Labor was much faster (even with Josh's giant head and shoulders. He was a 9 lb. baby).

After Dad completed his five year doctorate degree (which he did in four years by not taking any summer breaks), he moved Mom, Savanna and Josh to St. George, Utah, to set up practice. That's where my next older brother Colby and I were born. Utah didn't have the same laws or systems for birthing centers, so if a person wanted a "natural" birth with a mid-wife, home was the only option. Josh's birth was a more pleasant experience for Mom. Colby's birth was better still with a labor time of only ninety minutes. Now Mom was sold on having us kids at home where there was no cold steel or feet in the air while pushing against gravity. She was in an environment in which she was comfortable and in control. I am no history major, but haven't people been having babies at home for thousands of years until just the last hundred years or so?

It was a natural progression that when it was my turn, home was the place to make it happen. Mom even got more experimental and wanted to try a water birth. Again, I don't remember this, and I have to say I am glad, 'cuz if I did, I would likely be traumatized for life. The story goes that there were no complications. Did the meningitis have anything to do with Mom having meningitis when she was younger? Doubtful. Dad says 1 in 10,000 Moms have the dangerous bacteria in the birth canal. So one in 10,000 kids could be exposed to it. Of those, maybe one in 10,000 might actually contract and infection from it. I guess my number was just up. One in 100,000 chance, wow! What are the odds? Hospitals often take precautions by giving most Moms antibiotics just before birth, but the odds are so high just in nature, it seems a waste.

In case you are one of those people who don't know much about chiropractic training, or have pre-conceived notions about the profession, let me assure this, chiropractic school is hard and the training is nothing shy of medical school only chiropractors don't prescribe drugs. Instead of drugs they have advanced training in nutrition, the nervous system, and diagnostic imaging like X-ray. Chiropractors are basically neurologists who treat the body through natural means rather than using drugs or surgery. (I have to admit, I am thinking about becoming a chiropractor when I get older) Chiropractors are trained to be excellent at diagnosing and naturally treating what is within their scope and referring out to the right specialists when necessary. I can't speak for every chiropractic physician because after they graduate it is up to them to keep those skills sharp. All I can say is my dad knows his stuff and works well with a lot of M.D.'s, D.O.'s and other chiropractors who have their various areas of specialty. If Dad felt my innate intelligence, meaning the God given intelligence that runs everything in my body including organ function, digestion, immunity, you name it, would work best without the heavy metals used in vaccines as preservatives, then Mom trusted he knew what he was talking about. As you will see, it may have been an important piece in the puzzle of restoring my body to health, and now I trust him too.

# CHAPTER 5

# Hope amidst Handicap

When we arrived home, Mom and Dad's heads were both still spinning from the devastating news of the health challenges they would face with me. How would cerebral palsy affect my early development? What additional costs would our family face with my illness? Is it going to affect my schooling? Will I need a wheel-chair or crutches? Will I ever get married, or move out of the house? The future was uncertain as the seriousness of this youngest child's new health challenge soaked into their consciousness.

Dad kept thinking of the impression he had driving home, "Jay, you know what to do, just do it and be patient." What Dad knew is the same thing he has been doing for his patients . . . it involves four things:

1. "Blueprints" – by this he means removing any nerve interference so the brain and the body can communicate at 100%. He tells everyone that the brain holds the blueprints for the entire body and controls EVERYTHING by communicating with all the tissues through the nervous system. To help that, he "adjusts" people's spines.
2. "Building Blocks" – Dad says the food we eat provides the necessary "building blocks" to build healthy cells. I guess our body makes 300 billion new cells every day to replace dying off cells. If we don't eat good foods or have bad blueprints we will make bad or unhealthy cells to replace the old ones.

3. "Keep the toxins out" – If we eat, drink or breathe toxins, or junk, we also build unhealthy cells to replace the old ones. So, each of these three are important together.
4. "Give the body time" – This one is tough. My dad says, most Americans are 'programmed' to expect a quick fix. But the body doesn't work that way. Healing takes time. We can cover up symptoms with pills, potions and lotions, but true healing takes all four of these steps.

Dad has seen some pretty amazing things in his years in practice. People have gotten better from a lot of different health problems, even when he wasn't sure if this recipe would help. He tells his patients two important things, and they directly applied to me and my challenge as well. He says, *"ONE, doctors don't heal you and drugs don't heal you, so I am certainly not going to heal you. <u>YOU heal you</u>. My job is to remove nerve interference so your body can better communicate to heal itself. TWO, healing takes time. The longer you have been sick, or the more serious the problem, the longer it may take. The one thing I can't predict is how long it will take for a given patient, but I know the recipe works."*

Well if any case was going to test my Dad's faith and confidence in what he does for a living; it was going to be my case.

After arriving home Dad held me in his arm and looked me in the face saying, *"Okay little man, I am going to adjust you three times per week for eight weeks, then two times per week for eight weeks then one time a week for as long as it takes! Also, we are going to make sure you get the nutritional building blocks your body needs, while keeping out any and all toxins possible."* (Thus the vaccines for starters). *He turned to Mom and said, "Honey, since you are breast-feeding Harrison, we need to make sure you are eating healthy and avoiding toxins as well."*

Dad set me down and began feeling the tiny cartilaginous bones in my neck. He found that funny word chiropractic physicians use, "a subluxation," in the top bone in my neck. That means the bone was stuck, or not moving properly, which, in short, can put unwanted pressure on nerves and mess up that communication between the brain and body . . . my brain and body! *"Why have I not been <u>doing my job with this kid</u> these critical last two months?"* He gently adjusted my first neck bone, the one they call "Atlas," like the guy who held up the world. It wasn't earth shattering; there wasn't even a big 'pop' sound like I hear when older kids and adults get adjusted. But almost immediately after the adjustment, my eyes came down from being rolled up in my head and started to track on moving objects in front of me. Or so the story goes.

Dad is a big marshmallow! When I hear him tell this story he still gets all teary eyed every time. I have heard him explain it so many times, *"I didn't expect this response. And when I tell my other chiropractor friends or my neurologist-MD friends they all tell me, 'That is impossible!' My response to them is, 'I know it is but that is what happened. And if for no other reason, it gave me and Shannon a glimpse of hope that there is something we could do for Harrison. I just don't know how far we can take it or how long it will take.'"*

Thus began my long and difficult journey from the floppy-severely-handicap baby to where I am today.

# CHAPTER 6

# The Long Road to Age 1½

"Blueprints, building blocks, keep the toxins out, be patient." Over and over again that was Mom and Dad's mantra. It was Dad's recipe for success, and now I was the ultimate test subject.

The older I got the more obvious my cerebral palsy became. For lack of a better description, I was a "floppy" kid. I spent most of my first year of life on my back because I didn't have the coordination or muscle strength to do the simplest things such as sit up or roll over.

## Six Months

I was also still "extension dominant," or at least that is what Dad calls it. I just liked to arch back more than curling forward. It took about six months before Mom and Dad could hold me like a normal baby because I couldn't just curl up and rest my head on their shoulder, I would lean or arch back. Six months was the first time Dad could hold me this way.

At age 4-to-8 months most babies are developing motor skills where, when lowered suddenly, their arms and legs move to a protective position. Not me. When other babies are put on their

stomach, they scoot backward as they start to develop the ability to get on all fours and start crawling. NOT ME! I could not even turn over.

"Blueprints (chiropractic), building blocks (nutrition), keep the toxins out, and be patient." My parents were trying other things too, including baby massage, physical therapy, occupational therapy; oh, and definitely praying-their-guts-out.

### Nine Months

At nine months old I still couldn't even sit up on my own. Most kids at the age of nine months are able to crawl. You can see Grandma Fran holding me up, and my head seemed so heavy for my muscles. My dad tells me I had perfect little muscles, but the nerves were not telling them to contract cor-

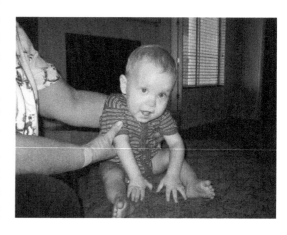

rectly. My muscles didn't have the tonus they needed. If someone put me in the right position, I could hold myself up in a quasi-seated position for just a moment. Even at this age I couldn't roll over to my stomach. I just had so little control of my muscles that I couldn't work them out in a way to strengthen them to do the simple things babies do.

Blueprints, building blocks, keep the toxins out! Mom and Dad tell me that just when they would start to get discouraged and think, "Ugh, this isn't working!" I would make what seemed a monumental mile-stone. They would remember the original prompting that said things would progress on "my time table," not theirs.

### One Year

At one year I started rolling over and quickly learned to roll to my desired destination. I still could not get up on all fours, so rolling was my new and best mode of transportation so I got really good at it. I could roll quick and in a straight line. That soon turned into a forward motion "tummy scoot." Dad calls it "the worm" and teases me that it was a Break Dance move. Mom and Dad would try to put me on all four limbs in the crawling position, but I would just flop back down and roll, or do, "the worm."

This is when a neurologist from the big city came to our little town. Our pediatrician recommended we let him evaluate me. Mom remembers vividly this doctor checking me over in great detail and confirming that I had cerebral palsy. He told Mom and Dad, "This boy will never run or kick a ball." He confirmed all the motor skill difficulty that the pediatrician had mentioned and then some. But by this point Mom and Dad had faith in the prompting and confidence in me and the progress I was making, all be it slow.

At a year and a half I could sit up, I could use sign language in full sentences to my mom, and finally I started to crawl! Dad says the cross-crawl movement of crawling on all fours is super important in development. He says, "It is both important in motor skill and cerebral development." I guess that means you need to crawl to help your brain develop right. This was a pretty exciting time in our family. Not just because I was showing off the early signs of my smartness by signing full sentences. And not just because I was finally crawling, which was a huge relief to my dad. But because Dad was selling his practice and our house so we could move to Europe. Dad and Mom had met a really nice Chiropractor from Portugal while they were at an International Chiropractic Association seminar in Greece earlier that year (2004). The chiropractor, Dr. Andrew Hatch, invited my dad to come work with him to open up a franchise of chiropractic clinics in Lisbon. Dad says he and mom discussed it casually before flying home. He was surprised mom would even remotely entertain the idea since it meant moving to a completely different continent and country with a different language. Mom had spent her entire life learning to read lips in English. Mom is lucky to get 60% of a conversation from someone she knows well who clearly articulated their words; a new country with a foreign language would be tough. Unless the natives of Portugal spoke English with little to no accent, Mom would be at a loss for making friends, or communicating at simple places like a grocery store.

Even with challenges of this nature, during the flight home from Greece to the States, Dad had a strong impression that he needed to look seriously at the Portugal option . . . so he did.

# CHAPTER 7

# Europe

Just a few weeks later, Dad made the big trip back to Europe, this time to Lisbon, Portugal, to meet Dr. Hatch at his office. Dad needed a better feel for the country, the business opportunities and the living conditions we would experience if we were really going to move there.

Everything felt right to my dad. Dr. Hatch and his office manager, Maria had a beautiful practice, not just aesthetically, but the way patients viewed and understood chiropractic care. Dr. Hatch was so organized and able to serve such a high volume of happy patients. The climate, the beaches, the history and rich culture at every turn. Dad knew that our family needed to be there.

When Dad returned and explained everything to Mom, he was beaming with excitement. Mom was incredibly supportive. So, our family literally sold everything we owned (at garage sale prices), kept just what we could fit in two checked bags and a carry-on per person, and transplanted our family to a new life on an old (new to us) continent and country!

**Cascais and Lisbon**

Within a week or two we were settled into a condo in Cascais, Portugal, the western-most suburb of Lisbon. Originally, it was a fishing village. Currently, it was an up-scale suburb of the largest city in Portugal, with a tourist flavor and a large population of foreigners, meaning spoken English was easy to come by in our neighborhood. Even the local theater played Hollywood movies in English with Portuguese subtitles.

Dad slowly began to notice little cultural nuances, like how everyone in the country lives within walking distance to a grocery store. The public transportation was amazing. In fact, a large portion of people did not even own a car. I guess the average European walks eleven to thirteen miles per day, where in America it is usually less than two miles per day. We had a car, but used it far less frequent than we would in the states. The sidewalks were made of beautiful cobblestone. Nice to look at, but oftentimes stones would come loose. We saw several people twist their ankles and/or fall just walking on the sidewalk.

I still struggled. My mode of travel had graduated from "floppy and practically immobile" to "awkward and hazardous to myself." The 'spills' were much harder on me in Portugal than in America. There was very little place I could play outside unless we actually went to a park or beach. Everything in our 4th floor condo was concrete and tile. Even the baseboards were thick tile like granite cut to fit with surprisingly sharp unforgiving corners. Just crawling in the home, I would really hurt myself and my head on the floor and tiled baseboards. When I started walking, the most simple of household fixtures became weapons-in-waiting to bruise, split or

otherwise injure my awkward and fragile body (especially my head).

When I finally started walking (around the age of two), I would often walk with the family, wearing a little yellow bike helmet, while holding someone's hand. Just living in Portugal with the sidewalks and the beaches, it was like natural physical therapy for my balance and equilibrium. I liked the beach. The sand was a much more forgiving friend when my "nemesis," gravity, would get the better of me.

One time Mom and Dad went out of town, leaving Savanna, Joshua, Colby and me in the caring hands of some family friends. Our friends left some cloths on the floor. Everyone was playing and I was trying to keep up the ruckus of their kids and my siblings. Slip . . . boom . . . ow! Head split open resulting in a five hour's wait at the emergency room (Seriously, a kid with a bleeding head, parents out of town and a five hour wait in the ER!?!) Thank you state insurance. I don't understand why people just don't take care of each other. If Mom was home, she would have made it all better. I mean, that is what moms do, when they can. Wouldn't the world be a better place if everybody was more in touch with their "inner mom?"

Anyway, Dad kept me on the same plan we started with: Blueprints, building blocks keep out the toxins and be patient.

### Organic Fruits and Vegetables

Dad talks about how much easier it was to eat healthy and avoid toxins in Portugal. Not that we can't do it in America, but TV, pop-culture and peer pressure sure make it tougher than in Europe. When we first arrived, we walked to the grocery store and Dad asked the produce guy, "Where are the organic fruits and vegetables?"

"What are you talking about," replied the produce man, "these are all organic."

Dad in a huff picked up an orange and asked, "Where did this come from?"

You see, Dad was still thinking American, orange plucked from a tree in Florida while it is still green, trucked to some other state slowly ripening further on the truck. Finally arriving to a produce store for sale a week or more later.

The produce man replied, "They are grown an hour out of town on the boarder of Portugal and Spain. They are trucked in fresh every other day." Our family had many experiences like this where we learned there are just different food standards.

### Chicken

Our favorite chicken restaurant was just a few blocks from our home. Mmmm . . . they made the most delicious "frango" (which is Portuguese for chicken), prepared rotisserie style. We could just walk over and bring a chicken or two home. The first time Dad discovered it he was walking in the area and smelled the most delicious food aroma. As his nose lead him to the restaurant, he found himself looking in a window with numerous chickens on the rotisserie, but he was shocked by what he saw vs. what he smelled. They were not very big. At first he thought they were scrawny like a cat. What is this? Rotisserie cat?! Then he recognized it was a bird so he asked the shop manager what they were cooking. The manager replied, "What, are you American? Can't you recognize real chicken (free range) from your American chickens all puffed up on steroids and antibiotics?" We ate delicious frango often.

### Fast Food

There were only three fast-food restaurants in the whole country (as far as we know in 2005-2006) and they were all McDonald's. One in the airport. One on the freeway near the airport, and one three blocks from our house in the heart of Cascais (remember, Cascais is a big touristy area). I think we ate at our local one all of three times in two years.

The regular restaurants were amazing! Every one of them we went to was like a home-cooked meal. In fact, one night Mom and Dad got back from a date and told us they went to their favorite restaurant and dinner was taking a long time. The restaurant was practically a tin shack with a giant tree growing right in the middle of it up and out through the roof. It was just a few feet (50 feet or so) from beautiful stone cliffs where ocean waves would crash below. Then they noticed the owner/chef enter the door with a bag of vegetables and items from the farmer's market. I guess he ran out of something and literally ran a few blocks over to the same farmer's market where we shopped so he could get what he needed to make Mom and Dad's dinner. They said the wait was worth it. Dad tells me it was so nice to learn how to slow down and enjoy each meal. In Portugal the people get offended by the idea of 'eat and run,' or fast food. They believe you should slow down and enjoy both the food and the good company at a meal. I don't know why, but in America eating is often times less of "an experience" and more of an "inconvenience." I guess in the working  world eating gets in the way of the next work project, so we just rush through it with so much fast food and junk food (at least that is what Dad says). As for me, while we were in Portugal I pretty much had to eat what Mom and Dad gave

me. I'm not saying I never had a treat or sweets; we just had to balance in more healthy stuff than treats.

Oh, and Europe has some fun treats and sweets. One time we were visiting Madrid, Spain, and it was a little chilly. We all sat

down at a coffee shop with outside seating. We ordered "hot chocolate" to warm up. Soon the server delivered cute little coffee cups with melted chocolate so thick we had to eat it with a spoon. Harrison's note to the wise traveler, if you are in Europe, you are cold and you want to order something to warm your bones, be sure to ask for, "warm chocolate milk" or like us, you will end up with something like a melted chocolate bar in a coffee cup.

We had lots of opportunities to travel and see amazing sites because everywhere around us was an adventure. From the beach at Cascais, to the Pina Palace in the Sintra Mountains, both just minutes from our home.

As time went by I was doing better and better. The recipe was slowly working. Keeping my nerves firing 100% with adjustments, eating healthy foods while avoiding junk and unhealthy things as much as possible. There were still plenty of times when Dad would carry me (most of the time if we wanted to get anywhere in hurry). I was getting better at walking and balancing, but I was still in need of a lot of help. Even though I was able to stand and walk some of my reflexes were just "off." When I would fall, my arms did not automatically react to catch myself. That resulted in injuries or bumps, bruises, and crying from a fall that any other kid would have easily caught their balance, or at least caught themselves on the way falling to the ground. Since I was just 2 ½-to-3 feet tall, it was still painful for my parents to watch any slip or fall. As if in slow motion, I would tumble helplessly, with all my limbs in all the wrong places to help reduce my impact with the relentless and rigid cement and tile floor. The slightest trip or stumble resulted in catastrophe.

Or so it seemed to me. My parents just kept pressing forward with patience, excited by even the slightest hint of improvement in balance and coordination. Hey, I was walking now, that has to count for something, *right?*.

## March 31, 2006

Mom had gone back to the states for a "Scrapbooking seminar," so Dad had all four of us kids to deal with for a few days. Savanna, Colby and I wanted a snack so we took the elevator with Dad down to the ground level, walked the block and a half to the store, got a few necessities and some drinkable yogurts (very popular in Portugal), then began the long journey (just kidding) back home. I guess I was "in one of my moods," or as Dad says, "You are ready for a nap!" Coming home from the store I was whiny and throwing little fits. (Hey, these are Dad's words; I only remember being a perfect angel). When we got to the elevator, the ground level doors closed on the shaft. Now this is important to understand. Many of the elevators in Portugal have shaft doors, but no doors on the elevator car, so you just stand back and watch the shaft wall go by. It is a little freaky at first; unless, of course, you are a kid, because your natural reaction is to touch the wall as it goes by and pretend you are Spider-Man climbing the inside of the elevator shaft.

My siblings had done that several times. Not me, I was too small. This was a small, six person elevator. Savanna and Colby were in the back, me and dad in the front. As dad stood with a grocery bag in each hand, I began to throw a fit, smacking the moving wall with my hands. It was a perfect temper tantrum up till the point I slipped. Dad reached for me, but it was too late and my left hand got stuck between the elevator car

floor and the shaft! Luckily for me there was a safety mechanism that caused the elevator came to a halt. Here we were, between floors, stuck in an elevator, me pinned, Colby hysterical, and Dad wondering how we are going to get out of this. Cell phones didn't work in the elevator because of the surrounding concrete, no one was answering the buzzer button, no neighbors could hear our screams, and Josh was just two levels up in our condo, oblivious to our predicament. Dad is no wimp, but he just couldn't pry the car from the shaft enough to free my hand. After my being stuck and him being helpless for over ten minutes, Dad went into something he calls "MacGyver Mode." I don't know what that means, but he started looking around for creative ways to get us out of that elevator. He took inventory of every-

thing we were wearing, the plastic grocery bags and the contents of those bags from our recent trip to the grocery store. Dad was wishing he had just bought olive oil or something viscous. No luck. But he did pull out a drinkable yogurt and think, "This is the most slippery liquid I have to lube up Harrison's hand." So he opened up a drinkable yogurt and poured it all over my hand. Dad and I together still couldn't pull my

hand free. He sat on the floor and put his feet on the wall of the shaft and reached between his legs prying his fingers between the shaft and the elevator floor, pulling the elevator away from the shaft giving my hand just a tiny bit more space. It didn't work before, but now that my hand was more slippery we were able to pull my hand free. Whew! I was finally free. Dad said, "The maintenance guy isn't going to be happy when he finds yogurt dripping down the elevator shaft." We were all pretty shaken up by the elevator incident. In fact, the only thing creepier or scarier that the elevator accident was the time we visited "The Church of Bones." Seriously, a church made of cement and bones!? Skulls, arm bones, leg bones, pelvic bones. Creepy. Who does that? And why?

I digress, back to the elevator story. So, in case you are wondering why I have pictures of the elevator story, well since we were all shaken up, Dad thought we should re-enact the event and take pictures to help us mentally work through it. You know the ol' "get back on the horse" trick. So, here is me pretending my arm is stuck in the elevator and then Colby freaking out!

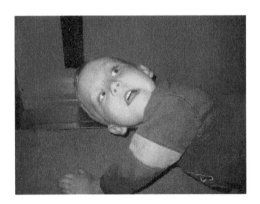 

The next part is where real trouble happened. As Dad sat at the computer looking at the pictures and journaling the story that night, an idea struck him. Tomorrow is April Fool's Day! So in an email home to friends and family he wrote up the entire story as it happened and threw in these picture plus a couple more. He just changed the end by saying something like this.

*"Dear friends and family the next paragraph is not for the weak at heart. Do not read further unless you are prepared for the gory and sad ending of this tale.*

*As time passed I realized it was up to me to get us out of here. No one knew we were here, no one could hear our cries for help, and my cell phone could not get a signal through this cement shaft. As I took inventory of the situation and what tools we had at our disposal, the thought came to me of that young man who was hiking in Utah and had his arm stuck under a fallen boulder. Eventually he cut his own hand off. All I had with me was drinkable yogurt and my Swiss army knife. I realized, Harrison's hand had to come off in order to get us out of here."*

Of course, his next paragraph stated that it was only an April fool's joke and he finished the story as it happened. He sent it out on April 1st to all our friends and family, but forgot to take Mom's email off the list. She received the letter while at her scrapbooking conference. During a break she checked e-mails in the business office at the hotel and could vividly picture everything in detail. As she got to the gory paragraph she was already in tears and couldn't read any further. She rushed out to the hall and sat down crying and feeling guilty that she was halfway around the world from her youngest child during this disastrous trauma. One of her friends from the conference saw her sitting on the floor crying and asked if everything was alright. My mom couldn't speak through the tears, she just pointed to the computer room. Her friend walked over and read the story in its entirety then said, "Shannon, did you read the whole thing?" Mom said, "No, I couldn't even finish it." Mom was already making plans in her head to buy an early return flight ticket to get back to me as soon as possible. Her friend replied, "Um, I think it is important that you read further." As Mom read on, her concern for me subsided and her blood began to boil as she thought about Dad and how she was going wring his neck when she got back home! In their ten years of marriage Dad had never played an April fool's joke, so she didn't see this one coming. Dad sure seemed extra nice to Mom the week she got back.

In late 2006 our family decided to move back to the States. Two weeks before we packed up, we went to the park. There was a nice park just a few blocks from our home, and we liked to go together as a family. It was a fun park with peacocks, turtles and a few other animals. It also had swings, kid toys and big green areas for people to run and play. Soccer is a big deal in Europe. Everyone plays it. All my siblings were running around kicking the soccer ball when I finally said to myself, I want to do that. I got up and walked out with the ball and started walking and kicking it at the same time. It didn't seem like a big deal to me, but my Dad sure freaked out and started filming it. He still gets pretty emotional when he tells my story because that was the first time I started trying to coordinate a faster paced walk and kick a ball. He says he was screaming on the inside with joy as he watched me and the neurologist's words sounded off in his head, "Your boy will never be able to run or kick a ball." I was four-years-old and still behind the coordination curve as compared to most kids, but I was making good progress on "Harrison's time," not "Mom's, Dad's, or other people's time scale."

# CHAPTER 8

# Home Again

We moved back to Utah, but this time the big city of Salt Lake. As we all settled into life in the States I continued to slowly progress. Savanna, Josh and Colby integrated back into American school. It had been a great experience for them to go to school in Portugal. Savanna and Josh even learned the language because they had to go to a regular Portuguese Elementary school. I think it made them instantly popular at school being international transplants. Colby just did pre-school for a short time before we moved back, so he didn't get as much language practice. Neither did I. I remember in preschool, this boy who would bully me whenever I went, so the first day I went he was bullying me after school for a while until Colby saw the commotion and he came over and stopped the bully. Every time after that whenever the kid harassed me, if he saw Colby coming over he would run away. I was really glad Colby was always with me! Colby and I were still home with Mom most of our time there. But now we were all integrating into school.

In first or second grade, I started playing soccer with a team, and during practice one day, I thought 'take that doctors! I'm running *and* kicking a ball!' My first soccer game against another team was kind of a bad starting game because it was *pouring* the entire game. Sadly I barely played because I hated standing/running in the rain. Practice was much more fun for me than actual games because people would barely pass the ball to me when we were playing against other teams. I remember one day at practice, my team did a game—half of the team against the other half. My team was doing pretty well. I was goalie for my team. A player on the opposing team kicked the ball at the goal. I jumped towards it to block it, SMACK! The ball hit me right in the face.

I seemed to do really good with school, reading, and such. Recess was supposed to be the most fun part of school, but it would usually be hard for me to keep up with some of the things my friends were doing.

I was moving along in school and little by little developing better motor skill. Dad had me try riding a bike with training wheels. It was awkward even with the extra wheels. I tried so many times without training wheels, but it just seemed beyond me to get that kind of balance and coordination. I finally told Dad I'm just not comfortable with a bike.

From time to time I would go for short runs with either Mom or Dad. I know I would slow them down, but I wanted some time with them, and I knew I could do it. Dad would mention little ways for me to focus on how to point my feet, or try to keep on my toes, or flat-footed rather than the heel hitting first when I would run. Little by little I was getting better.

In the fall of 2011 I overheard my parents talking with some family friends about a Thanksgiving Day 5K that would be fun to run and burn some calories before pigging out the rest of the day. It was a few weeks away and the couples were discussing participating together as families. The Altman's had three kids pretty close to our ages. I knew the other family was going to do it, but we as a family were undecided.

Shortly after that I walked in to talk to my parents and said, "Mom, I want to run a 5K."

They were both surprised, but thought if I was serious the upcoming Thanksgiving 5K would be perfect. We all agreed.

The morning of the 5K I was a little nervous. There were thousands of people at the run. I was there with friends and family. I kept thinking, "I hope I can keep up. I hope I don't fall behind and people get mad at me." When the 5K started it was really exciting running in a crowd of people that big. The energy kept me moving. The 5K went really well; I ran almost the entire thing! I hardly had to walk at all. I am sure the video is on my dad's website if you want to see for yourself (DrJayShetlin.com). I am the

Harrison - age 9

one who lived this whole story and when I watch the videos that dad has of me at one year, two years, four years and nine years old I can hardly believe the change myself!

I don't know what is in store for me but I do know that anything is possible! Dad says that a lot of people put limits on themselves where they believe they can only do a little something or can't do anything at all . . . and they are right! Others believe they can accomplish a lot . . . and they do! I guess we set our own boundaries of what we can or can't do. Well, I believe we can overcome a lot if we have a little faith. Even some pretty big physical challenges if we have faith, eat right (building blocks), get adjusted (blueprints), avoid junk (toxins) and are patient.

Dad says, *"This human experience offers everyone challenges to face, overcome or at least learn to deal with in a proper-positive way. Our challenges, setbacks, handicaps or injuries along the journey do not define us but our attitude and endurance does."*

Mom and Dad tell me that my possibilities and your possibilities are limitless!

What do you think?

*Harrison Shetlin*

# Today and the Future

By Dr. R Jay Shetlin, aka "Dad"

I have had the privilege of serving thousands of patients in my fifteen-year career thus far. Hopefully I am just getting warmed up. I have seen some miraculous health improvements through the help of chiropractic care and proper nutrition, but I don't think I have seen anything as impacting (at least to me personally) as Harrison's experience and story. One might expect that I became numb to it as the years have gone by and I have forgotten the earlier challenges, seeing him now as just like every other kid.

I still get choked up every time I share Harrison's story. **ONE,** because it is personal. There was so much time, love, energy and patience invested in this sweet boy by everyone around him.

**TWO,** because I see parents from time to time who bring in their child with a health challenge and will try something for a week. If it doesn't work they give up. Parents please don't ever give up on your children. The recipe works, just be patient. We are too programmed in this generation to expect the 'quick fix.' We think that if there isn't a pill, potion or surgery that will fix it, then it is incurable. – Don't fall victim to that trap!

**THREE,** because in 2009 while traveling with a medical team, "Healing Hands for Haiti," I had the opportunity to visit the poorest country in the western hemisphere. Our

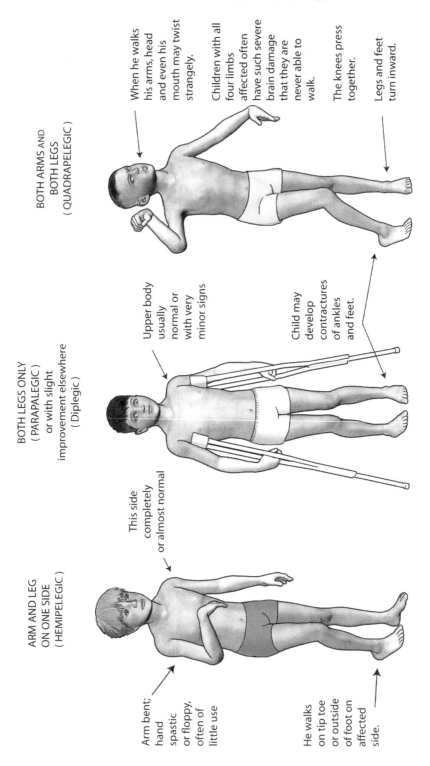

**BOTH ARMS AND BOTH LEGS ( QUADRAPELEGIC )**

When he walks his arms, head and even his mouth may twist strangely.

Children with all four limbs affected often have such severe brain damage that they are never able to walk.

The knees press together.

Legs and feet turn inward.

**BOTH LEGS ONLY ( PARAPALEGIC ) or with slight improvement elsewhere ( Diplegic )**

Upper body usually normal or with very minor signs

Child may develop contractures of ankles and feet.

**ARM AND LEG ON ONE SIDE ( HEMIPELEGIC )**

This side completely or almost normal

Arm bent; hand spastic or floppy, often of little use

He walks on tip toe or outside of foot on affected side.

team treated patients at the Port-au-Prince clinic who had lost limbs and were fit with prosthetics. One day we went out to the country-side to offer a day-clinic to a village without medical services. We saw everything from acid reflux to leprosy. On one of the days I went with a group to visit an orphanage. This is where something happened that impressed upon my soul the truly miraculous happenings of Harrison's life.

I learned that the culture in Haiti is, if a baby is "not right," some parents will just leave it on the side of the road or in the garbage. Maybe in a Christian, or other sectarian based culture, that would be unheard of. But the national religion of Haiti is Voodoo. I'm not depicting right or wrong here, just that there are cultural differences and legal differences in their country that are not criminal, but difficult for most of us to comprehend. If a live baby is found on the street, it is put it in an orphanage. Noticeably, many of the kids in orphanages are suffering with cerebral palsy, possibly born with the cord wrapped around their neck and that short-term asphyxiation lead to the CP. Regardless of how, a number of the kids in the orphanages have CP.

While visiting one of the orphanages we helped feed and play with kids ranging from toddler to fourteen years old. I had brought my chiropractic table to adjust some of the kids. One of the kids with cerebral palsy hobbled to my table with the classic walk Harrison discussed in an earlier chapter. The boy was maybe eleven or twelve years old.

When he positioned himself laying face-up on the chiropractic table, he was not able to straighten his legs fully and his arms were held in bent and spastic positions. His eyes were moving in a circular fashion, with a strong nystagmus. As he lay on the table, face up, I felt the bones in his neck. I could feel what we chiropractic physicians call "subluxations," or misaligned bones in his neck. Subluxations cause swelling that can affect nerve flow. If a nerve is pinched enough it will cause pain, but often times pinched nerves can affect our health without reaching the threshold of causing pain. Interestingly, with this kid the first two bones in his neck were really misaligned. I adjusted his neck and something crazy happened! His arms and legs straightened and his eyes stopped rolling around and began to track for a moment. It was like the kid went from completely spastic and mentally disconnected to consciously aware, grasping for some understanding (like someone who just woke up in an unfamiliar place trying to figure out where they are and how they got there) and his body temporarily had more controlled motor function. This lasted only for about a minute then he slowly slipped back into his regular spastic patterns. I looked at this kid in awe. I thought to myself, "Kid, I know your potential because I live with a boy like you. But with Harrison it took years, and we are only here in Haiti for a week."

I think of this every time I share Harrison's story, how this poor kid in Haiti is trapped in that body. If you ask your medical doctor "Is there a cure for cerebral palsy?" their answer will be a resounding, "No." I'm not convinced this is entirely true.

I certainly don't hold the cure, because healing happens from within. The body, in any ailment or disease, has to heal itself. We physicians simply try to help it along by removing nerve interference, improving nutrition, or, in the pharmaceutical model, subdue the symptoms with drugs while the body does its magic.

This much I do know, through the power of prayer and with natural means such as chiropractic treatment, good nutrition and avoiding toxins, the power that made the body was able to heal the body! I have seen it with Harrison and I have seen it in thousands of other patients with their varying symptoms and health challenges.

Today you can't tell Harrison from any other kid at school. With the obstacles he had to overcome in his life that is really saying something. From "The boy who would never be able to run or kick a ball" due to his physical disability to the boy who runs 5Ks and beyond, who inspires other to have hope, make healthier lifestyle choices, be patient and just believe, his is a message we can all take to heart.

*Dr. R. Jay Shetlin*
Chiropractic Physician

CPSIA information can be obtained at www.ICGtesting.com
Printed in the USA
LVOW02s0319021114

411082LV00002B/2/P